I Love This Dark World

I Love This Dark World

Poems by
ALICE B. FOGEL

Alice B Fogel

Z
ZOLAND BOOKS
Cambridge, Massachusetts

First edition published in 1996 by
Zoland Books, Inc.
384 Huron Avenue
Cambridge, Massachusetts 02138

FIRST EDITION

Book design by Glenn Suokko
Printed in the United States of America

02 01 00 99 98 97 96   8 7 6 5 4 3 2 1

This book is printed on acid-free paper, and its binding materials
have been chosen for strength and durability.

Library of Congress Cataloguing-in-Publication Data

ISBN 0-944072-64-X $11.95

Fogel, Alice (Alice B.)
I love this dark world : poems / by Alice B. Fogel. — 1st ed.
p. cm.
ISBN 0-944072-64-X (alk. paper)
I. Title
PS3556.O277I14   1996
811'.54 — dc20   95-43971
CIP

The author wishes to acknowledge with gratitude the editors of
the following magazines and anthologies in which these poems first
appeared:

Atlanta Review, "Ripening"

Beloit Poetry Journal, "Grassfire," "Which Way the Winds Blow"

Boston Review, "The Necessity," "No One There" (under the
former title "This Afternoon"), "Still Life With Woman"

Conscience, "Unfinished Poem"

Granite Review, "What Rises"

Greensboro Review, "Permission"

Lungfish Review, "On An Afternoon Sleepless in Bed"

Out of Season (Amagansett Press), "For David, the 'Bubble Boy'"

Ploughshares, "Beholden," "Grief"

River Oak Review, "Returns"

Third Coast, "Parhelion"

What's Become of Eden: Poems of Family at Century's End
(Slapering Hol Press), "The Safest World"

Witness, "Barbed Wire"

World Letter, "Fishing," "See, the Smell of My Son"

"The Necessity" also appeared in *The Best American Poetry 1993,*
edited by Louise Gluck and David Lehman.
"Permission" also appeared in *The Women Writers Calendar 1996,*
edited by Dena Taylor (Crossing Press).
"Beholden" also appeared in *Hospice Magazine.*

I am also grateful to the poet Lysa James for her helpful comments
on some of these poems in their early drafts, and to the artists
Fran Beallor and Deborah Kruger for their frequent and fecund
discussions on balancing life, motherhood, and art.

Contents

for Mark Edson
who hears the music and the meaning

Unfinished Poem

(After the Michelangelo sculptures, each called "The Captive,"
often referred to as "The Unfinished Sculptures.")

I'd imagine my way out of the stone.
First, I'd test every surface pressed against mine,
every edge and angle that I'm up against.
I'd test texture and position, concentrate
on solidity and weight. Inside, unseen,
the stone is smooth and cool, the same
as my own skin. I can't define myself.
Below is a deep, frozen river,
where I've stood since time began.

Now—I want to get out.

I've begun to imagine how an arm would feel,
straight instead of bent, or a muscle, slack,
not pressing, not lifting, not pushing or resisting—
what an arm would do, free to rise by itself:
I've begun to believe in it.
I'm sure I remember the sculptor's hands,
now gone to dust; my own body is still alive,
whole, the way I was imagined if not made,
the way I was found, and captured.

I am breaking for the utter sensation
of air and space and time, where nothing
is etched in stone, where the memory of stone
is a surface tension snapped by will:
a skin. Now my own arm, lifting
only against itself, the up against the down,
not against this dead weight. Yes,
I imagine myself, surrounded by all the blades
of air: unsheathed, unshielded, ready to be mortal.

Eidetic

for Fran Beallor

Nothing happens in the still life, except
for this: the essence
of its chosen parts, themselves
lesser than their sum.

Each item—mask, cloth, surface, box—
has a history, a language, archaeology
of secrets. Listen. Light
at once falls and returns; shadows
fade between angles. Arrangements
have been made and carried out.

Layers of time link like lyrics
for a song, rising through the medium:
time framed. While the artist worked overtime,

time stood still for her, just as now
it does for you in viewing. Fit
your life inside it. Art comes to life

when the eye invites its intimacy,
joins it. Time and again
you'll look at the picture—the same, all in all,
but all at once changed.

Something hidden emerges, something aforethought
recedes. How like life, the way it moves.
So let yourself be fooled;
you don't know everything.

For instance, you can't see,
in looking now, that this amaryllis
lay long dead before the kimono
and the lamp were set beside it,

or that the brightness of open windows—
visible in the high gloss of the vase—
diminished and rose in countless repetitions,

and the orchid's petals opened and dropped
as the artist's brush stroked them.
See how, with patient attention,
for each petal that falls,
she returns it to its stem, time after time.

Meanwhile what she had in mind
is still reflected in the ardor
with which textures embrace each other,
stand aside, or touch.

And in the miniature self-portrait
cupped around the contour
of a bowl's mirroring sheen,
she has left herself the room
to stay quietly inside it, even while
her life goes on.

Ripening

Nothing but time—when it is time—
can make the blueberries ripe, their skins
plush as lips, deeply filled with the colors
of bruise and breath and bliss.

Nothing can rush this, this slow swell
of growth, this lush and lavish splash
of fruit, this bloom and blush and burst.
You can't feed it anything to speed its time—

nothing generosity or economy, hope or desire, can do.
What softens them is all that, too, can soften you:
the length of days spun by the wheel of sun and moon
the same way one continuous thread becomes a cloth.

Like the reviving trees in spring, or astonished flowers
emerging from unfrozen ground, these blueberries
feed on light. Light is their cue and key, the same thing
that feeds me what I know and do not yet know but will.

Because I eat blueberries in midsummer, I like age,
the news it brings of things I've known well all along.
I like the questions it poses, and the slow
but sudden way it replies. All the while

I have been too busy to wait, I have been waiting
for this, and this, and this: each successive,
deliberate day. Through the wild plenty of time,
nature's pace is a walk, a mild ramble

over mountainsides and fields. Who remembers berries
in November? I want to forget nothing, miss nothing,
but then—the trees fall away in windblown, broken strokes
and let in newer light, and there is still more to behold.

Now, all summer, we have been patient and excited,
almost a year since we climbed our home's hills with our fingers
combing the green for its deep-sea blue. Here, the blueberries
will ripen in the third week of July, no sooner—not even

if cities are built in a day, or swords are beaten
into plowshares. There's no hurry, no hurrying them.
And when they come, after the equinox, after the fireworks,
after all, I will roll each one in my hands,

name them, and count them each like blessings.
Then with my tongue I will parse and split and swallow them
so they enter the bloodstream all red and blue because now
is the only time.

Pattern

Standing to one side, like an edge, the trees
reconsider the distance. Movement comes slow.
They form a line, a pattern. Nothing is as it seems.

Against the dark a silhouette of dampened leaves
impresses the bark, and on one branch a crow
standing to one side, like an edge, the tree's

last blackened leaf. The better to see
across the twilled field, it flies in low
lines, in a pattern, or so it seems.

Like messengers, the crows in twos and threes
reconvene in the trees, swaying to and fro,
standing to one side, like an edge. The trees

drop their seeds on the open hills and lees,
blown by random winds, and weather, and the blown
lines form a pattern where nothing is as it seems.

What tends and sows is the same breeze
that mows the meadow so trees cannot grow.
Standing to one side, like an edge, the trees'
line forms a pattern: nothing is as it seems.

This Time

Still frame. The deer
is a presence
like spring, like fall,
unprecedented.

The deer moves like trees move
in storms: of necessity,
heavy with grace, somewhere
between forever and a moment.

Her head swings slowly
like time, forward and back.
Then, stillness—a flattening
of dimension, a sudden sepia.

Now the deer shifts
to life, bends her neck
to windfall, lifts to fruit
left on limbs.

Each time the deer stops,
rocks roam freely in the field.
Each move redefines—revives—
the landscape: aging fences,

browning leaves, the brittle
perennial reach of weeds,
just as each day
tomorrow is renamed.

But the deer's pauses,
made of listening,
bathed in patience, are tools
that sculpt surrounding space,

meant to lead us to dusting
leaves, moss growing
on stones, the flit
of our own lashes.

Now she looks right at us,
we think she sees us
but her evening ritual
continues, careful,

a tension acutely becalmed.
Deer, those apples are free.
Our breath etches the glass,
our eyes sting

from the effort not to blink,
not to let go this time.
The deer stands as if ascending,
as if always, as if casually

poised to leap.

Sea Gull

Needle, icicle, flash of eye
           in light   this swift
  shape of white
            caught me in its wing-
span out-spun, overhead,
                inland.
It traced a high arc
           sparking winter sky,
  sewing its sharp
           quick stitch
on raised eyes'
         air   and carved
a new design at the darker
              edge of sight
  across the slower beauty
             of an unmoving
afternoon moon.

The Nelson Bog

There never was a thing so crystalline and colorless,
steeped in every form and shade
of a single element called silver gray.

Twilight at any time of day: say afternoon,
say March, a warming trend close down below the air.

The bog loomed like fantasy — the water silver gray;
the ice, silver gray, floating along surfaces —
the only horizon between water and silver gray sky.

The sky hanging like wet moss in densest mists
over steaming ice, and reflected — below, above, within
the water — a silver gray wave of air like smoke

diffusing the diffused.
And finally, brush-stroked, the trees

a silver gray more darkly impenetrable,
less lightly mirrored, rising up from a fog like parishioners
too moved to speak their prayers.

Instead

Where I see nothing instead
  the dragonfly sees its own flight,
    the waves its wings
      throw through the atmosphere
above the pond. June. Sunlight
  jewels its thirty thousand eyes,
    whole worlds possible
      in each one. The dragonfly
seizes the air, every molecule
  an object of mercy or reckoning.
    Water seethes in the air's embrace,
      condensing, evaporating,
between pond and sky,
  between eye and eye.
    The dragonfly—mythical, simple,
      weightless Pegasus—
sees the throb in the throat
  of humidity, the expansion
  of atoms, suspension bridges
    spanning every hue.
Think of the refraction!
  Think of prisms, how the dragonfly
  hovers between rays thick as mirrors,
    conspicuous as neon—
finds its path through forests
  invisible to me, in one square inch
    of light—witnesses the air
      as it flies up into futures
blue or cloud, or falls
  back to the pond, still cold from the spring.
    The dragonfly rides the train
      of tomorrow's rain

down the rails to a taste of blackfly.
  The waltz, the hunt, the loom,
    the dragonfly's ancestral dance
      and the weave
of actual time and physical space.
  There is so much that I don't know.
    The dragonfly knows ash and dust,
      pollen, insect, seed and scent,
light, lightness, shadow, shape,
  the lift and swoop and race of wings,
    last year's disintegration,
      next century's tree. Tonight
I could look up into a summer's night
  and see there this life
    before it existed, and after,
      and instead.

Fishing

This is how we'd speak,
I'd be talking to you now
from the low lilt of wooden hull
in water, to the curve of lure
hooked in the mouth. Or would,
if you could hear
through your deep loneliness.
All along, trees step down
to the edge, lean waterward, curious
eavesdroppers. The return
of reflected light
graphs the shape of their timber.
Rocks hold their breath
just below the surface,
waiting for some contact.
My only regrets—
that my line is finite,
that it isn't effort but grace
that sends it out as far
as follow-through allows.
I catch something whispering, green,
inedible. I catch the glinting hiss
of solitary steel, the winding
in harmony with wind.
I don't know how to resist,
to stop reeling in the line like this,
hypnotized by the pull
of drawing somewhat nearer.
In and in and in, the sound
of the circular, the pause
before the sweep of rod in air,
the sigh of breathing out.
What I care about

is this sequence, the repetition of rolling
inward over and over, then the turning
aside, the casting out again,
the chance of lengthening my reach
with this one string between us, musical.
Then strumming the golden lure, looping
back through the resonance of waves,
the fluid echo of loons
thrumming on the gunwales.
Quarter-moons of silver fish
would stitch a fine horizon,
sewing lake to sky, weaving me well
into its net, safe between the lines.
I would rise and fall
on the tidings of nights and days
you could count on in your sleep.
We would never have to speak.
You would have heard that silence
lacks nothing but words.

On an Afternoon Sleepless in Bed

The moth at rest is a window
of patience. Its meditation
is better than sleep.

Here, tightly folded, safe
in their compression, three moths,
three small spears, slash
seeming cracks in the glass.

Even in this heavy afternoon
the grass stirs, trees are alert,
beyond the inert, dark, aloof dash
of these. But a fourth

unfolds its inkblot symmetry—
wings, sideways, widely awash
with filtered light.

This is a studied stillness,
that of whole hours, dreamlike.

This is the flutist's breath held,
the suspension of a time; a waiting
that especially loves itself.

Still there! Watermark
floating on the waning day,
stain that takes your contours
and shapes, transparently, to heart!

A happy parody of flight,
this feat of affection: that one
could cuddle into glass
as I do in my counterpane.

No One There

The sun is setting elsewhere in the woods and I hope
that no one is there to be struck
by slant rays or shade or by the sight
of trees rising in her own thoughts—I hope no one
is bearing witness to his vision or the damp whispers
of molten leaves under snow—this afternoon
whether a ruffed grouse or a hawk or an owl
lingers, lucky, in the eaves of a sunset,
whether footprints spray the snow with shadows
or the branches of dead oaks burst through the air—
I hope that no one is there
to dream about solitude and language
and the coming on of night.

Which Way the Winds Blow

What hand opened the door, I don't know. No one
lives there in winter. And I don't know if it was for entrance
or for exit that the place opened itself, or was opened,
though I do know what boundaries
were broken. The lake lay frozen, the sky
still as folded wings. And everywhere snow

blown into the rooms, strewn across the braided rugs
and knotty boards, under chairs, creeping
like a slow cold tide, white and silent, out of its element

with greed. Then I remembered the photograph,
black and white, as old as me or older. What eye
watched that scene, taking it in, shameless, I don't know,
though I do know that boundaries were broken:

A woman, her grey dress blowing toward land,
lost on the shore in the dim light of her long day's end,
and a man, farther up the beach, alone. The sea—
mute, infinite entity—taking in its borders hungrily;

and the stolen child it drank up when each
entered the other in a moment
of dropped vigilance. In this kind of world no blueprint

instructs us how to house what we love
against the winds of loss. The woman, the man,
their child gone—slipped from the safe home of their love,
swallowed whole. I am not going to try to feel

what that woman felt, or to speak with her voice. I don't know
what she did next or how she did what she did next.
She is the mother, my fear, all the love ever lost to grief.
Her pain is an ocean vaster than planets, a diaspora

of longing flung to all four flogging winds. In her life,
I am sure that time drifted past her, with her, within her.
I know that that summer, like all summers, moved on
through the fall into winter, that the shore closed up,
abandoned, cold. And that the thing lost

still blows through us, the swollen door no longer shuts.

Surrender

for my daughter's birthmother

How beautiful is the lost: shoreline
taken by clawing waves / snow
melting into mud / spring erased by heat.
How losable what we desire / love.
Oh yes, she will be beautiful
when you lose her / when you give her
away, she will lose you when you go on
tunneling through the heavy element
that is your life. You will hear your own cries
as if from some distance
and not know which, of all the choices,
hurts the most. And yes, it hurts:
things breaking apart / things extracted /
things detached with scissors and knives /
things left behind. Body from body.
It's like a death, this being born.
You break in two — each half
heals whole again, division and sum.
You can do this, go on, take this life / give
this life, a belonging to believe in. You will
bear all this and live, walk home alone, walk
into the curve of the earth, that one embrace
that holds you, rocks you, keeps you
from going too far / from getting too lost /
from falling off: a place to fit in.
I hardly know you, nor you me.
What we don't know that we never forget.
What we live for / without.
What we will lose / surrender.

For Anica

To love is to die
and live again and die again . . . .
          — Octavio Paz

It isn't the same, I know, what I learn yearly from gardens
and what you learned from city streets this year
before you were three. Not the same to clear the ground
of yet another obstacle, and to be born in this world
to a daddy who was black and now is dead.
Every day we perform the impossible tasks, cast aside

any rocks that fit inside our two cupped hands.
Watch for daylight and delight in it, its daily bread
and conversation, what it asks of you, the way it demands
that you work with your whole body on this earth:

even in the emaciated smear of that winter light
that crusted the place you stood upon, in the deep
     abiding freeze
of loss, under the desolate sky whose sun you don't
     believe in.

Maybe you wanted to ask the sun — take me with you
over the edge tonight, down to the other side — take me
     with you,
I don't want to rise. But you never ask,
you go back outside, you rake away the stains
and shove your nails beneath the surface where corpses
of ancient souls have left for you their jeweled debris,
     and there

you take the leap of loving one more time, one more stab
at life, plant one more seed that grows in dirt
under the knives of rain, the stroke of lightning or luck.
And you watch over it for all you're worth, because this
    world thieves
like erosion, thickens with ashen wings, scavenging.

And in time you'll see what it gives back to you in kind,
the choices you are left with, everywhere another chance
    given
to love today, the chance once more to raise your sights and
    aim for it,
to aim for the heart, to risk the obvious.
And it grows, it grows!—the stem, the leaves, the season
    to live,
and you stand there flowering, small and powerful if only

for this once. Anica, I think I understand the garden
and the story about being shut out of paradise.
I think I see how every life at best
is an expulsion
from its last brief stay of happiness. So you get up

again, if you can still move at all.
You pull up the dead stalks, you crush them, push
    them under,
turn them loose into new dark rich soil, you jab
your fist down into that deep moist dusk, again and again,
your little fist full of grief and rage and seeds, and if
you are really, really lucky you will get to be
thrown out of the garden again.

Permission

Tenuous white tendrils, these new roots, keels
on the stems of pussywillow sticks stuffed into a jar.
I see now that they have balanced you for a time,
in a place, between death and life.
Every week in March I tried to wade through the snow
to bring you home, a sign of spring. Finally in April
I could lift my legs high enough over the field
to steal your little puffs of growth. And now
that I have come to throw you back outside, I find
this new life under water. So you have stood in the window,
inert, at first, like a seed, not dead after all— even sprouting
new body parts, learning to live again.
This must hurt, like the rapid and shooting
growth of babies' soft white bones. And this latency,
this ability to plunge into, to feed on, whatsoever element
will take you, amphibious: Of course I am jealous.
Because yes, I will dig for you yet another home,
on this side of winter this time.
You will be permitted to feel the dirt as it enters,
surrounds, every delicate, raw nerve of root and branch.
You will be allowed to remember the long stems, the family
of stems, the air that supported you, and to forget
the months of still, cool water, necessary and cruel. You
will know the deeps, the buried earth, eat it, and be free
to come to life again.

For the Dead Man

It is not unusual to hope
that you'll stand out—if at all—simply
for who you are, and not, say, for having
worn your bedroom slippers to the game.

Maybe sometimes, in the crowd,
you paused for a moment,
weighing a need for belonging
against the evidence of being alone.

Everyone else went home.
Later when they found you in the bleachers,
you seemed to be deep in thought, still
caught in the difficulty of the question.

Grief

I am ashamed as I try to sleep,
counting the wounded and the dead
in this old day's news,

the grieving ones they leave behind.
Counting stones and bullets, averted needs,
the pretty breaths of my family beside me,
counting on a world that I don't trust
to keep my children safe.

What was I thinking? Did I forget those others,
the rubble of their troubled worlds
and mine? Does it fill their days—

their remembering? Or do they remember too
to choose their favorite breakfast bowls,
that red dress, the time to step out of doors?
When I lean my body over the fragile forms
of my husband and children, I am afraid

I am not strong enough to bear
the grief of so much loving, the burden
of our survival from day to day,

or of what we can't live without, but will.
How each of us fends off despair—
that is what we are made of
when all else is dust or luck.
Each stranger's grief is not my grief

but it lies under everything, like ice.
Sometimes I fall through it.
Sometimes I walk achingly.

I am not saying their voices rise
above the hum of comfort here and now.
I'm saying I believe that even sweet blue skies
will break away, leaving nothing
between my eyes and the face of a god

who says, Look down into that dark place,
meet your own shadow there.
Go on, take it, take it on. Grieve:

Go down into the dirt.
I want to have already known its taste.
I want to have swallowed it alive.
If I fall asleep tonight,
if I do not die before I wake,

what will have lifted me back to perfect
that other thing that we call hope
is more love: the leaven of all sorrow.

Without Weapons

And then today, without weapons aimed, it was
possible to see this: the loon, turned loose
upon that lake, slowly turning west,
south, east, its sweeping glide
more sweet than any scythe.
The ellipse it offered up

behind it — ever widening — encompassed, in its wake,
even me. And the reminder, however much
a question too, that anything so beautiful,
moving about so gently, rapt, oblivious,
could exist here in this world,
in this same world. . . .

For David, the "Bubble Boy"

David, heaven is too much
like a glass dome.
You call it home, that unfair
equation, sorry syllogism
of spheres not permitted to intersect.
Outside in: yours
is the prison that guards freedom,
where outside equals death.

Life at all costs, life above
all else, and life
more than anything on earth. For a time,
like another child's lightning bug,
you breathe in the overturned
world of a jar. You might as well
stand before blind gunmen,
the bullets' chances of finding you
as great as God's germs'
queued up beyond your round walls, waiting.

The weight of safe hands, or a mother's
owning embrace, are these
the best of love? Does it come down
to only this? That silence
falling beyond the walls is only the wind
curling endlessly over and over.

You want to go to it, to travel freely,
like blood through the heart. But
don't go, David, into that open room,
your last white bed, the living air.

Coyotes

It was a long, sharp harmony and it pierced through the dark
into every corner of wood and stone and air.
It cut through the window and stabbed my sleep,
which bled a little through the room.

I was awake before the sound had died away, but barely.
I heard only a sort of reverberation of sound,
so that if I worked backward through it
I could reconstruct it whole.

I sat abruptly up, trying to know where I was.
The silenced echo of that howl
was a raw hand that shook me; it was fear.
It was a waiting that could wait forever,

that drew me into its conspiracy. That night
the coyotes never did return, but every morning
is an intake of breath
rimmed with their lost note.

The Necessity

It isn't true about the lambs.
They are not meek.
They are curious and wild,
full of the passion of spring.
They are lovable,
and they are not silent when hungry.

Tonight the last of the triplet lambs
is piercing the quiet with its need.
Its siblings are stronger
and will not let it eat.

I am its keeper, the farmer, its mother.
I will go down to it in the dark,
in the cold barn,
and hold it in my arms.

But it will not lie still — it is not meek.

I will stand in the open doorway
under the weight of watching trees and moon,
and care for it as one of my own.

But it will not love me — it is not meek.

Drink, little one. Take what I can give you.
Tonight the whole world prowls
the perimeters of your life.

Your anger keeps you alive —
it's your only chance.
So I know what I must do
after I have fed you.

I will shape my mouth to the shape
of the sharpest words,
even those bred in silence.

I will impale with words every ear
pressed upon open air.
I will not be meek.

You remind me of the necessity
of having more hope than fear,
and of sounding out terrible names.

I am to cry out loud
like a hungry lamb, cry loud
enough to waken wolves in the night.

No one can be allowed to sleep.

Catena Mundi

Everyone has seen how the dust falls,
hung, as if by chance,
in a rope of light; how it seems,
sometimes, to be rising
back up to heaven.

And the refraction of light
seems a curve of joy whose rise
never equals its fall, a catenary
inadequate to complete
connection of earth to sky.

Still, standing on the bridge,
it is enough to live
for the sight of late day's light
sinking into the river
and yet rising to our eyes.

Sunk deep within is the desire
to see our fallen neighbors hung
and let the popular channels televise
death by painless injection.
And this is not the end.

In inventing a god we created
shame, the fall, and the other dream
of rising. From the heart
extends the evil of despair.

And yet the same source sustains
the instinct, the grace, the urge
to reach one's hands across, to place
them on the wound: involuntary bridge.

Poem for the Old World

And now I have given birth to sons,
and sons of a Jewish mother are Jewish.
One is named for my father's father,
who came from the Old World
to raise his American sons. And now I,
who have never once gone back,
I think: All of this—this only world—is the old world.
Old in its infinite list of births and griefs,
its heavy wounds, its thick silt
of guilt, old in its terrible forgetting
and its terrible memories,
especially the memories that live on in our cells.
Our cells will always know—know of death,
mostly, life, some. Soon all the elders
will be dead and who will be left
to remember the last time
it came around in this old world?
I will remember. In my bones
still shaped like theirs, my bones that still
could seem to pierce through my shrunken skin,
if it comes around again. In my blood
that looks for the places to hide, to try to survive,
if it comes around again. In my voice
hushed in warnings insensible to children,
silent warnings because I don't want them, yet,
to be afraid of what always has come around
again. And yet I will want them to remember.
People say that things have changed.
I have changed, my father has changed,
and his father is gone, though his name
and image still live on in my home.
First seeing his new grandson, and hearing
his own father's name, my father asks his question

and hears the answer hard. He has memories
of his own, and regrets. But then
he says, my father says, *Well good, then,*
don't circumcise the boys; maybe that
will save them, when next it comes around.

For America

On the couch till late, through blued glass,
I watched foreign skies on the news.
Here, ours rose so silently through its dark trees
and dusk, it seemed to float unmoored.
I listened for its promise of sleep as I bowed
over each child in his own bed, safe.

Unspeakable, secret quiet, broken only
by the click of my lamp as I darkened the room.
And in that black instant I turned up my face
to the skylight and the sudden
shock of sky fell in like the thunder
and bombs over Baghdad, blazing with shrapnel and fear
that traveled faster than light. Nightmare fireworks
exploded in that molten sky while under it
my two small boys and their father
breathed the same, as if in peace, and my own breath
imploded and opened me like a wound.

America, America, my broken heart
sang before her billion brilliant stars
grew cold again, and simple, in the night.

Surviving the Accident

Here it is, you say—calm, unaware
of voicing the words. . . .
And then a time, lengthening,
new and attuned as birth. Struck,
you go mindless, notice
you are beside yourself:
that must be what's called the *soul*,
standing aside, waiting to let go.
Now the body moves, mundane,
discarded, with nothing left to contain.
It floats forward as if winged,
listening to the glass
ring in your windy hair.
The slowed world changes shape.
Shadows tunnel you toward light.

It doesn't matter; is, perhaps,
of fleeting interest.
But to see your death up close,
to be brought to, and turned from,
such a lit and open door—
this seems a mistake.
Like a child's glass-encased snowstorm
after the indifferent shake,
your own little world
rights itself and settles down.
A silent snap—the soul turning back,
the body now refilled:
small miracle of normalcy.

Back home, lists in your own hand
tell you what you would do that day.
There are still phone numbers
of people you wanted to keep.
Your plants are still in bloom.

You find evidence of a particular means
to a precarious happiness.
When you recognize yourself,
in this moment, for just one moment,
you wish that you had died: finally,
all the need might be absolved.

Each night, the crash reverberates
like waves of nausea.
Solid metals melt and move.
It's only now, awake, remembering,
that you remember to be afraid.
When you were going to die,
other people were daring to decide
what they'd have for dinner—
as if believing we're all safe.
We are never safe; but also I know—
though I don't know why or how—
that every single day (until that one day)
mysteriously, indefinitely, instantly,
we are saved, and saved again,
and once again, saved.

Still Life With Woman

In every room there is a woman, palpable.
She takes object lessons from the inanimate.
In the scene, she holds a large red pepper, its skin
taut over muscle and a secret, subdued core.

She has shaken it like a child's rattle,
and now contemplates its reticence. Her knife,
a fine tool, lusts for the chance to split
its shining stillness, its infinitude.

On countertops, windowsills, patience piles up
like the sweet dust of mourning and time past.
Shadows spread from under coffee cups,
stopping short of overflow, the way voices

reach in toward her, dissolve unheard.
She is like vegetables, like china, smooth, clean,
unconscious of the myths of tableware, fables
of toys, studies of form and change and form.

What does she feel? She feels red pepper,
paring knife, chance. The way she is actually
poised in the midst of things:
wood, glass, light from above, this life.

The Lightning Tree

After each storm, I step out into the world,
once again upon a time, and see it turning
into something too wounded and beautiful to touch,
although I long to.

When I climb Silver Mountain, I lose myself
at the lightning-stricken tree, just yesterday
lit up by a single chance reckoning,
and now at once dying and smelling of birth.

Fresh storm-cut boards splay outward from a core
still standing like the pistil of tropical blooms.
Even now, its terrible report splinters me,
nails me to the ground of my own backyard.

I pace the borders of my own life
like an immigrant distrustful of home.
I fear the twisted road of time, the open
spaces it travels, even deep in soothing woods.

If I could dream myself back as far as the reaches
of remembrance, find the moment of severance,
I would thread that knowledge back
through the eye of here and now. Always,

I am like the newborn, whose own newness
struck and opened me. His soft head,
pungent as first dust-damping rain,
draws me down to a tenderness like despair.

Why can't I love him bravely, fearlessly?
My embrace is drenched in pain, thundered
with cries of loss, electric with regret.
I am dangerous, but love keeps wanting me

alive, on this mountainside of blueberried air.
A lifetime ago this was all pasture;
now it's ripe for harvest with trees,
each insisting on the pretense of permanence.

At the peak rests the old planetary carpet of rock
and sky enough to break the boundaries of states.
This high northeastern world unfurls in trees,
encircles me in waves of gray and green.

Up here, it is a vibrant repose.
This room, that is not a room,
never echoes the sound of living wood splitting.
Awash with wind, it blows open every door.

Learning to Read

I remember when each word was a tiny drawing,
the perfect work of art: ecstatic carvings,
exotic lines, simple curves conducting
an inaudible opera on the page.

I remember suddenly knowing that my mother
didn't see the black markings, their meanders
through white valleys; she saw sounds,
even things: she saw a boy, a boat, a tree.

Now, at 3, my son's letters are still mobile,
unleashed to direction left to right,
and without pedestals—like Inuit sculptures
meant to be held, every which way, in the hand.

So a 3 is an E, W is M,
why must there be a 6 and a 9—they are one
and the same. Learning to read—
not even meaning to—

we tie down the forms, tell them which way
to go. They lose most of their freedom
while we gain much of ours.
Loving the story, his hand caresses the paper

with the same yearning tenderness as mine
smoothing hair from his brow—
as if he could touch what the words say,
as if he could feel in his hand the world

that speaks to him so strangely
with his mother's familiar voice.

In my own old, best, repeated dream
I float down a river on an open book,

reach the greening shore in spring,
and hear the Mother Voice call my name.
It is the voice of earth and sky, sailing,
blowing through the leaves of the book.

It is the voice of the home
where I want my son to go
whenever he leaves home.
Whenever he learns another word,

every gain of his is my gain
and my loss, every celebrated step
full of mourning for its footprints
left behind. My hands, full of joy,

pause in their applause, positioned as in prayer:
Please, don't grow up too fast. Words,
those broken twigs, those forked rivers,
those unpaved roads, will carry him

away from me, to other lives.
There is not enough time to hold him
without holding him back—the way I could
in that brief time

when meaning had no name.
Even these words, carved so deep and hard
by the circular motion of my hands,
can never spell out enough love.

The Sunflowers

So sated, with sunlight, summertime, and seeds,
the sunflowers bow down their heads.
Made of only bone and soul, I am a darker thing.

While my foolish tears have nothing to breed,
those seeds are boats that sail back from the dead
to be sated again with sunlight, summertime, and seed.

I can't forget the babies who could not breathe,
that what might keep them alive was neither love nor dread,
that, made of only bone and soul, I am a dark, dark thing.

Don't tell me about sunflowers, redemption, faith, or need,
about the balance of day and night or of darkness wed
to the sated, to sunlight, to summertime, or seed.

I have seen the cruel gleam of this world's teeth
in my children's darkened rooms. Listen, I said,
they are only made of bone and soul; I am a darker thing.

Fear sobs in my head when I'm too far from them to see—
as if the cord has bled, as if they were already dead
and sated, with sunlight, summertime, seed,
bone, and soul, and the darkness in everything.

The Safest World

Darkness is your silk scarf, a soft disguise inside which
    you hide,
little one who takes cover, who loves closets and curtains,
loves to hide without being sought, and lie still,
somewhere inside somewhere, in pleased silence.
Inside you is the memory—I carry it for you—
of a darkness darker than pre-birth.

Now you reach so gladly to close yourself in, a re-birth,
and before the door closes I witness the smile you think
    you hide,
which is all for you, for the embrace of air that you
gather against your face. Or under the bed, its curtains
of fabric down, hems brushing floor, you crouch in silence,
not waiting, suspended in some deep, some still

unnamable pleasure, and there you will stay, as still
as moss in shadow, and for as long, until the birth
of satisfaction releases you from out of that silence
or some other kind of hunger sends you out of hiding
to find me on the other side, so strangely free of curtains
or shade, under the beam of burning lamps that you

like to leave. In your secret places, deep sea treasures, your
patience is as infinite as the dark, your heart still
pulls your blood through tunnels warm as bedsheets, and the
    curtain
of your breath waves invisibly, in and out, like birth.
Darkness is the anchor trailing daylight, following—but
    first hidden—
in day's wake. For you, a place of peace and silence.

I want to bridge my arm through that silence,
through your own dark passing of time, to offer you
an arc of twilight, a road opening across the high
pitch of night, a pier to the rise of a future day that I still
insist upon. But you hold on to the darkness, giving birth
to it with both hands. You stay behind your curtains,

and I don't know—should I reach in past the curtains,
should I "find" you, pull you back out of that silence,
and hold you close again, body to body, just like at
    your birth,
your small self full against my longer one, so that you
might remember the world of solid arms, the hold in which
    you still
fit, the one I have for you? Or should I let you hide,

trust your bright curtained eyes, full of the excited peace
    you hide
like a secret from birth?—as if the safest world for you
were this dark and silent one you will make as long as you
    still can.

In

We lay down these pathways, long planks, as bridges
across the force of gravity. This field
looks like a smooth field of grass—too smooth,
we notice—and no cows graze on it. Their skeletons,
we are told, swim heavily down below.

In the land of earthquake, volcano, and this quicksand,
we move cautiously. This long, pretty lawn, cleared
mysteriously from the craggy rocks and woods,
is a mud as thick as mercury, a flood
of solid earth. Step on and you step in.

If you walk out on the board that takes your weight,
stamp down on the splintering wood, you see waves
buckling the acreage, and feel the friction of your shoes
shifting over your feet. The whole dictionary of earth,
air to zenith, liquid to solid, embraces this strangest place.

It smells of honey and creosote, something thickening,
unclear. What lingers or hesitates down there,
invisible or forgotten?
Depths resonate, depths sing and call
for sinking down, for falling in, for overwhelm. Depths sound

a dreadful music in minor key, a beckoning.
I shake the long plank. This emerald meadow is so tempting,
such an invitation to immerse. Something
powerful wants me, something that says: Fall in.
And feel the softness of this moist soil soothe your skin:

Let it in.
I want to risk it, to see if I can dive in, even swim,
to see if I can work with it, artist and medium.
Let me see how long I can hold my breath in,
tight and hard and swelling against my bones,

so it takes the shape of that room inside those walls
outside of which flow the quicksand and the overarching
bowl of sky. And when the time comes to let burst
that breath, like an earthquake to let it asunder.
I will sip in the wine of this steepened earth.

The Rapture

They tell me if I go down
any deeper, into the depths,
I'll never rise alive
from that unlit place.
Close your eyes, they say, to deceptive
blues, and to the booming movement
of the element. Don't imagine the sweeping
breadth of its being.
                    I dive
even deeper, through architecture
of splintered edge and fluted grace,
through the emeralds and pearls
of precious inaccessible air. I dive
as if heaven were down there.
I fill my clothes with golden silt.
They say I take too much.
            In the shallows, they're afraid
I'll drag them all down with me
through the shadows of my rapture.
I begin to dance, I believe
I've found my own evolution
among the sodden, succulent weeds.
I open my mouth to sing
to the white-sided creatures that roll by,
and the air I swallow tastes like blood,
thick as sunken treasure.
                    I even laugh
as my new weight carries me so far down
I remember the old lullaby
I heard once in my sleep. Later
I will rise to the surface where the furious
tension bursts as I break it: my own
divine intervention.

Returns

Listen, even the earth says it wants to rearrange, empty
its lungs and fill the sky
with relic, fossil, bone. The earthquake, the volcano,
have their roots at the stillest center too, and bloom
at last as if a lifetime later.

And still you call a rock a rock
and mean unchanged,
when it is the stone that lingers for nearly eternity
before it crystallizes, all the while so carefully
embroidering the rare and breathtaking

minerals into porphyry, looming on for eons.
Whatever is the matter, it is the world's
own blood flowing, purled, that finally pulls upward toward
the surface, which splits, singing, from within:
open, molten, then solidified again. You know the way.

After any inspiration, what gets taken in waits,
then breaks outward, awakening into the shock
of resurfacing, the home it had forgotten, the fresh
and stinging air. Something new replaces the displaced.
That's how stones live their woven lives.

So, in time, any time now, the whole of it will explode.
Solid air, surprised, will welcome and make room
for what it had once let go, the way the sky
accepts the offered blossom
of a whale's sudden breath now exhaled.

Beholden

Still I am not sure which is most vivid—
the love now risen from its previous absence,
or the future loss it rides like a shadow,
the eye's after-image of a bright light gone.
In any case, with its harrowing blades,
this fertile line of love already
draws through me a beautiful symmetry:
the invisible, downward reaching of dark and buried roots,
and the opening, airing branches that they mimic.
Always, love is something coming to an end,
something that could die before its time
and so you live in it, a world, a frame,
the borders that define. You memorize it,
day by day, like the lines of the earth's face
mapped and changing, mapped again and again
changing, over centuries, the impossible
becoming true before you. And like that,
you look for the shapes of things now being
that once were not: no matter
how you hold a day, it sets into the year,
buried, lost. In memory its sheen
is another branch. We see that coming.
It is precisely that passage, that change, that tunneling
through the soil of time—that dread—
that makes love what it is: so rich, so far
beside itself with beauty, beholden to it,
because it can never be held.
It's just that love is the highest point, the lightning rod
that draws to it the crooked path of sorrow
which it waits for, depends upon, uses in advance,
not the way that we use air—of necessity, for life—
but, instead, the way that birds use air:
for balance, unbalancing, uplift.

Home (Angel)

Now that you
                    are asleep
I lean far out the window
          on this   the ground floor
                    of heaven
and there is no
          sound
                    in the infinite
shades of darkness
          save the clouds
stepping lightly over the leaves
    and the insects
                    keening
          in thin air
like blood thrilling
                    in the inner ear
of night—
          all those tender wings
slipping through spaces   lately
    left open
                    by your laughter.

Host

I hope to make you feel at home, always.
In the fall, you moved in, then in winter
moved inside me daily: reverberation of a love
I will recognize every time I see you.

I am rehearsing the exact angles and shapes
of your still-invisible face.
When I see you, I will know it.

Meanwhile, your new, increasing strength
makes the shifting of warming snowdrifts
seem mere echo of motion in womb.

While you sleep this round of seasons,
little mollusk, we dream you
to life in quickening gasps
that rock you on your ocean floor.

Drifting sailor, deep sea dweller, be my guest:
I promise you your shell, shelter, breakfast.

See, the Smell of My Son

See, the smell of my son
 is as the smell of a field which the Lord hath blessed:
. . . of the dew of heaven,
and the fatness of the earth,
and plenty of corn and wine. . . .
            Genesis 27:27, 28
            (Isaac speaking of Jacob)

Smell of harbor, berth, the open sea
Smell of buried earth, salt, slow moss
Smell of steamed rice, tall grain under skies
awaiting impending rain
Smell of self balanced beneath blankets
and tethered to sheets, weighted by the sweat
that wets your hair into halos
Smell of dust dampened by sleep, humidity
rising from bone and blood
Smell of the deep inside you
Smell of your skin, your white arms,
tiny, fine, and able
Smell of your temple, smell of your lips
Smell of bitter herbs, sweet breath
Smell of animal and garden and fog
Smell of sorcery and forest
Smell of darkness and day and bedtime
and air and sun and wondering
Smell of seem and be and birth and body
Smell of your smell, your floating room
Smell of cocooning, echo, bloom

Letting Go

No wonder he laughs—the ceiling is gone
and opening like song. This is new
and he never pauses or looks back
but crawls off toward edges
wherever they may be.
Ten months, and he's just found that onward feeling—
the falling, flying breach
of being born to spring and bodily motion,
the joy of stepping out of doors,
the quick, iambic, heart-beat two-step
of a breathing body displacing space:
Look at him go, safe at a distance.
Earlier this morning, at my breast,
his concentration was as fixed.
His eyes peered at my close skin as if it too
were infinite. He knows no better.
From him I borrow his oaty, newgrown smell,
his spring-rain skin, his cool-water taste.
His mouth is a warm, strong place
where words are yet unborn.
When he is full, he shifts backward
and a line like a spider's silk
blooms between my breast and his lips.
It is beaded with the diluted
saliva'd milk in his mouth.
Wet thread, as clear and strong as the water
of waterfalls, it changes me like waterfalls
change the rocks they travel by. I watch it lengthen,
this waterfall, this web, this thread of life
between us. I hold him—and my breath—
both dearly, and I tell his eyes:
This is how I love you, this is how that love
trembles with its tiny musical notes—pearls

of our bodies; this is the warp and weft
that weave you to me loosely, the gravity
that never releases us even when we let go.
This is the embrace that holds as lightly as the sky.
He is listening. I carry him outside.

Seeds

Jake stands with me at the window.
Nuthatches, grosbeaks, bluejays
scatter an early spring breakfast
of seeds all over the ground.

"Chickadee," he says, his word
for birds and for seeds,
and he points to the boxes of seedlings,
eye-level, on the sill inside.

He wants to watch like this every day,
to see coiled leaves unfold at the soil
and rise on their single slender legs.

How like them he is—new, surfacing,
dangling upward in the air
as if drawn there by hands or rays or light.

Seeds project their futures in green
unrolling through anything—whole tons
of dirt, rock, knitted older roots.

With atomic force, imperceptibly,
they reach through the dark in search
of a home for their instincts.

And rising above the soil,
they bear down into it,
breaking it apart, braiding it together,
for balance and for strength.

Jake grows as fast as the seeds
in our tiny window garden,
and he grows the same way—his way,
which is any way he can:

by heaving aside or through or against
the stubborn or the swayed.
He has his own element.

His hold on his world
is as loose as soil, as essential,
and as rich.

Awakening

Listen to the calling of the wood
hushed to ashes in the stove,
the shuffle of pajamaed feet coming our way.
Listen to the sheep wanting their feed,
the quick patter of lambs
already at play.

Hear those morning-bell harmonics
of sap springing into emptied buckets,
the hurry of wild things
peering from snow and trees.
The sky arches blue, just out of reach,
brushing by when our backs are turned.

And we, without words, touch
each other, one by one,
moving through thin light and rooms,
held aloft, still at home, and rising
to another day, new weather.

Weather

The more intimate we are with weather,
the less we question anything else.
Birth, death, age and change,

the helplessness of rabbits in an owl's talons,
the evaporation of wet cloth on the line.
Life is in the melting pawprint of maple leaf

I see each winter in snow, the way the snow
cups itself for warmth beneath thinned leaves,
supports the trunks of trees, smooths the steepness

of hills. Weather saves the important things.
For sons and daughters come again the arrows of ice
softening into tears, come again

the lush and the pallid, and the twisted trees like those
Moses must have seen, when he argued with God
to be kind. Now, with this new birth in spring,

everything is as clear as the snow when it melts,
as clear as the spreading green of new leaves,
as the pond skimmed with dragonflies and the air

one coming October day. I could grow old
happily, looking at my world like this, at each
of you in it, every month of the year.

In February the wait. In March the chance
of running sap, birds spreading seed in April
and the drying of heavy mud brushed by wind.

Then the plantings, and blankets for late frost,
the tending of growing things and mending
of fences, all with the touch of the artist

moving through galleries. August's warm stars,
September's tomatoes and moons, the autumn
harvesting of daylight, color, and food.

The sleepy cold of December, mice running
through ice tunnels into the changing year.
Weather says everything changes, and we know it

with comfort, not fear. Always, the same way,
we talk each year of the differences: Remember
that wall of snow taller than a man, how early

the blackflies came last year? Everything
is precious in continuance and in brevity,
in the sureness of its presence while it lasts,

how it seems to burst upon the scene, and how later
we remember its slow fade. Newest child,
you are the same in how each day, like weather,

you are different, your very cells, the sentience
of your eyes and tiny hands. I love you
for how fragile you are, how close to the surface

that edge of mortality waits, even as you grow.
There is nothing tentative about you, or about
my gaze, which sweeps you in like a tidal wave.

What secret storms will cloud your blood,
what old reigns does your breath recall?
Small blue veins rise on your skin

like shore birds lifting off from above your eyes.
You will not remember this, that I stood watching,
counting your lashes as they grew like evergreens

on a far hillside, when the June sunlight
clarifies every line and shape with heat.
You will not remember a time before the seasons

had gone around enough times for you to know
the meaning of their repetition and trust
their sequence with undying faith.

Spring

you come made of whole cloth, like a child,

familiar unfathomable. I can't take my eyes
off you. Spring, spinning spun
of patience urgency, electric mild,

you are a new life
better than mine, less afraid, less induced
by fear, more sloppily insistent, more happily unabashed.

How blessed you are,
you do not call yourself by human name
or count your days in numbers.

I call you
a way of life, intricate plain, and fervent.
You reach down

around and through me, and needle the snow,
and underneath its quilt
come forth the green tongues telling

their one secret, memorized always new.
I overhear it; I believe it.
I wing on the breeze like blankets

left to fly off the line. Spring,
you befall me like child's play
and I fall for it every time, every

last moment of you. Your commandment
never balks, never passes, it can't wait.
It arrives with forewarning out of the blue,

woven out of winter hurtling toward heat,
glacial eruptive. Spring, my favorite one,
you are a time,

you are noun verb, you are a weight
that gravity can't take. You evaporate
age from my pores, the way April

dries my hair in the plush loft of its air,
as if you had offered your arms and taken up
in your many hands the weak, the wet.

Oh, I am grateful
for many things, but none more than this:
this unownable gift of life

and I will save it just as it saves me,
for when this brief season goes
I will catch its last thread unraveling,

I will sew it onto the wind,
I will pass it back through my heart.

Unlocking

But it is not always quiet here.
Things go on while we sleep the sleep of soldiers.

Ancient branches crack and splinter into dust.
Large wings snap open in spring
like carpets splayed out over the railing.

Granite splits apart at the seams
and great animals cleave roads through woods.

Daily, in the density, there is life
on the edge of the knife that cuts the world
into hemispheres of sense and death.

Trees are born and die, bones turn to humus,
glaciers to meadowland. It is time

to turn yourself loose, like new leaves,
like big lakes on which swim enormous birds
at a distance deeper in breadth than the water's depth.

Their shadows pull you to the shore.
Their size fills your lungs with sky. It is time

to heave aside the boulders and the dams,
to come back out like a bear after the thaw, to be
ready for the forest, for the forage, for the full

and waning moons. You will get soaked in wet grass,
feel the insects pierce your skin. You will learn

to balance between gravity and light. There will be
hot and sticky nights, sharp songs at dawn,
long and bright ineffable days.

This is your chance to crash your way
through underbrush unlocking like so many doors.

Grassfire

Here it comes again, drenching sweet grass in flame—
like a conduit, the traction of a deep breath
sucking in every air like undertow from here to there,
untangling from the undergrowth, fast and hard and high.
Here the fire, hurtling like a boulder hurled through space,
hurting molecules, ripping apart atoms, exploding
like a blurted secret. There is the taper, the point, the coil:
what it all comes down to: unraveling,
blowing up into vastness. Arrow of fire, wounding.
Red surge weeping and more redness swept
over this injury, this blame, this absence of grass.
But look, I think I could be
swimming, diving down defying the element
that would consume me, turn me smooth as clay, burn me
to tender ash. I could wade in to these waves
and float through that color, that heat.
And perhaps with my hands I could draw the thunder
of this wild grassfire through the field, urge it on,
entice it on to the pond for its denouement where it hisses
its one last sigh. Our eyes are filled with small black wings.
Let the wind rage, let us now come clean.
Yes the grass is singed; let it grow back, bright green.

Explanations

Reasons rise the way mountain ranges rise
from ancient oceans and bedrock.
How else to explain this shell I find,
intact, along a high inland ridge,
but that glaciers once spread from sea
to shining sea, carrying their cargo of silt,
salt, weed and shell, from eon to anon?

And once, this mountain, born like a shocking
new idea or a sudden memory of pain,
exploded from the deep-and-buried—
first rattling its underground chains,
then, subterranean, the cold earth slipping,
colliding with austral lands, sliding skyward,
crushing boulders and raising aloft
whole green seabeds like shaken sheets.

Violent change is true today, here on a narrow road
all winter lifted like a hero on the arms
of expansive gestures. It's early spring,
the road heaves stones up out of the frost,
hurling rocks through schisms
that weren't visible yesterday.

Every day now, afloat, new stones
are surfacing like trout. I know
water expands as it freezes,
fills the hints of air between
each grain of sand and another.
And ice dissolving in springtime seeps,
released, alongside the pockets and pathways
of its own slopes. After storms, too,
the landscape reconstructs itself:

like the great hurricane of '38
that lifted the past back like ghosts—
arrowheads, coins, old foundations
bursting through such century-soaked mud.
What is lost to us is not gone but buried. It lies
like the unconscious beneath blankets woven
for darkness and for warmth. We go on, in time.

What if the explanation for upheaval
were simpler than we could ever know—
not like something rising like steam
from some implosion below, not the breakdown
of breadth, a plummeting toward death,
not rebirth, not the flagrant
quake of a molten soul from which
blood like lava flows.

This relic, for instance, this once-lost shell
from some other life that rises now to my eyes.
It is curved like a newborn palm in mine,
scalloped, pinked, and tinted just like daybreak.
Small, hard thing, still smelling of salt,
and telling of a time—the season
when wheels and wind and footsteps,
and sunlight simmering down,
compress and change the land.

Maybe its transportation too was simpler—
not glaciers but, in winter, a truck
full of sand and salt shipped like spice
from faraway seaports. And all this comes to me
because I walked here today, on this road,
over this mountain, through this life in spring.

Barbed Wire

Before I had children I walked through the woods
beyond the pastures, where last century's fences
were once pushed against the bark of some young trees.
I saw how the trees had grown swollen around wires,
swallowed them and gone on ringing with their age.
I followed one wire to its disappearance
centered in a maple, as if it were incidental,
and I found where it emerged, clean, on the other side.
Sometimes the trees grew far and rich above the cut
hardened and healed before memory could stoop down
to listen, those branches in the sky oblivious
to this blemish, this gash, still visible at the level
of a child's eye. But I was not thinking of children then,
their soft flesh, impressionable, nor how fast
they grow around us, how miraculously tall
I have become.

Changing the Story

All the children I once was
begin to burn onto the horizonless dark,
faces and hands visible as white coals.
They ask for me by name.

They gather, older holding smaller.
Some say it is time to speak.
All of them can cry now, and they cry
in my name. Listen to me,

says the nine-year-old, locked in the dark
for three weeks. Me, says the baby
whose mother didn't know how. One
calls out from her frozen dread.

I say I will listen, and the sounds
hail another kind of darkness, lightning-
flecked. My ears sting
with the bright sparks of their rage.

I envy them their cries, their heart-felt,
age-shattering need, the joyful way
they know how to ask for me. And I listen
to my true sons, too. One says,

Change the story today.
Make the blue jay sorry, make the babies fly.
Where does the sky begin to be blue?
Mama, I love this dark world.

I know so many children who make believe
that they are grown-ups, who, in turn,
wish to go back to a dream
of ease and simple pleasure.

So many grown-ups who make believe
that they are not children
who grew up to forget how scared
and lost they were, without crumbs

to follow back to any safe and loving home.
How hard it was to understand
anything: monsters, magic, the swinging
of moons and moods. I remember.

All these children won't let me forget.
I will stay and tell them new stories—the many
little dark-haired girls, the two living boys,
all of them open-faced, open-handed, waiting for me

to rise up wholehearted from ashes.

What Rises

You are someone I've always and never known.
Nearly extinct, anonymous, you are
like the bird that knocks at my window at dawn
and falls down at my door.
Where should I look,
where shall I direct my eyes?
This accident is not mine by rights.
And what if I do touch it, what will the smooth spoon
of my palm mean to it—more pain?
That's what it is like with you:
something stunned, panting for breath, dying
to fly away. Sister, I know that somewhere
there are white moons rising in your skies
like resurrected birds. When you believe it
you will see: there is much in life that rises
from belief. Sure there are laws of the land,
air, gravity, but we can live with that.
When you meet yourself on solid ground, finally,
your shadow becomes you. It is a light
and airy thing. Even fear lifts wings.

Archaeology

I live in this miracle of walking on land:
deeper than oceans, its waves of clay and sand
carry me. Layers of old leaves and time,
leavings of other deaths and lives. Leavening.
Sponge of humus, clumps of stone,
tiny wildlife — on these we float:
on loam upon loam upon loam.
Soil is our source and destination: home.
Civilization, Atlantis, insect histories:
this year, again, buried treasure helps to feed us.
Easily moved, easily lifted, by weather, shovel, hand —
so easily earth supports me. Primitive, thick,
original every day: a heritage of sweet dough
handed down the generations. This spring,
the garden plot lies down lightly underfoot,
and tolerates my work. It is good
in my fingers. It loosens my fist like relief.

Traveling Light

If you look closely with all your grief
you can see the scars casting their shadows
on the landscape. The miracle is
that flowers still bloom here at all.
Some of us stay up late fingering catalogs—
ixea, freesia, alyssum—
imagining the flowering of earth.

We'd make it work in the old way
as if diamonds grew from grime, and stones
bore fruit, as if anything could ever
change so much, or be strange enough
to love.

Once when I was small, I laid out bits of ribbon
for birds to weave into nests. Silvered yarn,
colored thread—I cut them carefully,
arranged them along stone walls.
I wanted to be kind, to love the world
the way that I knew how, or the way I wanted
to be loved: with gentle attention,
offerings from which to choose.

Then I saw, in the tree, that bird
broken, hanging
from some pretty string I never told anyone was mine.

Now what I want is to understand everything
for the mystery it is, and love it simply
for being my world—
to suffer the witness of it,
to touch the ground as lightly as flood-risen stones,
to touch it as if not at all.

Roots

I remember, we breathed water:
air came to us in disguise.
Then memory began attaching
its own vast reaches
to the not-yet human
imagination.
Some earthlike mass was where
we next went crawling,
dragging prehistory like seaweed
on useless gummy feet.
Now, we pretend to be complete.
The old rhythm nags at me,
wants to take me back
where things are never said
to solidify with time.
On the surface, even islands
may seem rooted,
though it be
to something unseen and oceanic.
All it is, is, they know
to stay aloof, aloft, afloat
in just one place,
treading water
in secret down below.

Forgiving the Darkness

Darkness is not a death, does not obliterate,
will not bury you or take your breath away.
Darkness will not erase you the way it erases day with night
because darkness is not the clock but merely the time
falling away from the clock's circular face.
Darkness is not the loss but the thing misplaced,
not the hammer but the nail in its curved emergence
from wood's grasp, not the storm's insurgence
but the limbs broken off from their miraculous
suspension in a storm out far, beyond us.
Darkness is not about hearts, imperfect as they are,
but what leaks through their incorrigible doors, nor the stars
but the glissade or glide of their dust.
Darkness no longer shields the hunters' musk
in search of you, or turns you to animal prey,
it is only a measure of weight or days.
Not something without a beginning or an end,
it is not even—especially not—an end.
Nor is it vertigo, nor the whole, but merely a piece.
No, darkness is but a ghost of an idea, the least
remembered, most estranged prayer, and your fear
but a lingering, limbic fear torn from shreds of forgotten years.
Only that much is clear.

Echoes

Flat against far walls there is always a sadness
waiting to be felt, waiting to hear its name.
You call out to it and—good company—it answers.
You find a reason—the sadness enters it
like swallows swooping through barn doors.

Every open space lies between the boundaries
of bodies: parent, lover, mountain, room.
I have heard the sounds that rocks and hills
throw back at me.

When the tilted leaves, for instance, whirl upward
before rain, what happens behind my tongue
is like an aperture clicking open, open,
until the mouth has carved a cave for words.

Now I listen for some echo of organs piping sound
from hollow suites, repeating beneath my own skin.

Long before buildings, sidewalks or streets,
the wild landscape met its occupants halfway.
The pigeon was a parrot in full color.
When the world grew gray, so did its feathers.

Now the city bird mimics the walls that house it
and only its sleek neck reflects the spectrum
still invisible in the sky. In my throat
I form a word, take it back, let it go.

In the beginning: my mother calls me in for supper.
I answer her with her own words and tone.
She sends out my name from the back kitchen stoop;
I return it from the front yard.

Between the gray pavement of Justamere Drive
and the gardened walls of my home, I learn
to fill my small life with whatever I am given,
and then pronounce its sounds.

Alice? Alice. Where are you? Where are you.
Question and reply, demand and counter plea.
Come here! Come *here*. I can match myself
to anything, one-to-one, world to word, a window
through which brightened birds take flight.

Parhelion

I saw the sky blow open from its center. I saw
the whole pasture bow down, like a ship before waves.
The sky began to expand, circling outward,
from memory toward prediction, in rounds of muted hues.
The damp air invited it, suppressed it, led it on.
Clouds — grayed pools of fingerpaint — spread,
collided, and splashed over mountainsides,
while planets swept along in spindrift until angels
fled their halfbright moons and rings.
If it went on like this, on a normal day,
the sky would vanish, leaving only the unbearable gaze,
the utterance of fossil and bone, the jagged edge
of broken sky in its complicated darkness,
and my own jagged edges, no longer eclipsed.
Always, I thought, there is a given, unempirical —
for instance the world, born from out of nothing,
the truly immaculate conception: an absolute
in direct relation to nothing. Barren galaxies
breed a trillion tons of stardust in a teaspoon.
So anything I can imagine is possible, anything I dread.
There are seashells in the hills, sundogs in heaven,
absolute good on earth — I believe it.
And what is beyond dream or horizon is on its way
back home. I call out to it. I expect it to answer.
The world is time, running in circles, catching its own tail.